Leader Insights
Leadership Essentials to Inspire and Guide

Dr. Corcy Pruitt

Leader Insights: Leadership Essentials to Inspire and Guide

By Dr. Corey Pruitt

A Publication of ChangeSparx, LLC – Phoenix, AZ

All rights reserved. No parts of this book may be reproduced or transmitted in any form or by any means, electronic or mechanical, including photocopying, recording or by any information storage and retrieval system, without written permission from the author, except for the inclusion of brief quotations in reviews.

Printed in the United States of America.

Copyright © 2024 ChangeSparx, LLC

All rights reserved.

ISBN: 9798339553496

DEDICATION

This book is dedicated to a handful of leaders who have inspired and guided me through the years.

Coach Darren Richie

Dr. Chris Bustamante

Captain David Plucker

Dr. Patricia Case

Kenny Ruhter

Terri Plucker

Dr. Kate Smith

Gabriel Barrientos

Adam Brooks

Butch Liston

Lee Loyd

Roger Whitmore

Jim McCormick

CONTENTS

1	Dear Leader	Pg 7
2	Attitude	Pg 13
3	Motivation	Pg 19
4	Accountability	Pg 25
5	Coaching	Pg 31
6	Feedback	Pg 37
7	Collaboration	Pg 43
8	Trust	Pg 49
9	Support Self-Efficacy	Pg 55
10	Change	Pg 61
11	Influence	Pg 67
12	Radical Improvement	Pg 73
13	Model the Way	Pg 79
14	Cast Vision	Pg 85
15	Notes	Pg 92

1
DEAR LEADER

Dear Leader,

I do not know who you are, or how you came to acquire this little leadership pamphlet.

I do not know what education you have either formal or informal. I do not know your gender, or race, or color, or religion. I do not know what circumstances, experiences, or person lead you to this moment in which we find ourselves...This moment in which you purposefully and intentionally expand your leadership.

What I do know is that you were destined for this moment...for this collection of leadership insight scripts. Destined for leadership greatness.

What you hold in your hands is a collection of leadership insight-scripts. A small collection that was passionately curated through decades of research, miles of travel, trial and error, and the fortune of apprenticeship under numerous mentors.

These insight scripts you have before you are not just some words scribbled on a page from some unknown narrator. Rather they are absolute truths, dare I say laws, that govern - and have governed - and will continue to govern, how effective leaders lead others. They are lessons taught from some of the greatest minds - minds that, if I revealed their identity, you would quickly recognize. They are lessons that continued to surface across academia, religious texts, philosophical texts, across various art forms, and found in the secret musings of effective leaders across the globe. These insights are *NOT* meant to be exhaustive, rather, they are triggers to start your leadership contemplation on the subject. And, hopefully, will lead you to a deeper unique understanding of leadership.

But, dear Leader, heed this warning. If you begin this journey, it will change the way you lead others. You will not be the same. But, this is the point - if you are not growing and changing, you are decaying and dying. This is an immutable law of nature, to which humans are not immune.

Here is how you are to engage with these insight scripts:

First…
On Monday of every week, read one script and read it two-times over. But, don't read it just as a "task" to start your day. Don't read it for knowledge only. Rather, read it to understand it.

You see, dear Leader, this is where many make a vital error in their leadership growth. They may read a book about leadership, or a passage, or wise commentary, and they move on to the next. They expect a one-time passing of information will lead to behavior change. They expect a one-time passing to suffice.

True change, true personal impact, true influence of the information will come when we allow the information to seep into our consciousness and invade our awareness. It is then that we move past knowledge to understanding and understanding to action. It is through information acted upon that we realize what we have truly learned.

It is through information acted upon that we realize what we have learned.

Second...
Return to this week's script each morning for the remainder of the week, allowing the leadership wisdom to sink into your actions.

It is through spaced repetition that our mind moves information into long-term memory. And, from there, we are able to recall it and use it at will.

Don't pass on this critical step, as I assure you, this is where true leaders begin to separate from mere leader-actors. This is the step, dear Leader, where the mystery of leadership influence is revealed. This is the step where your unique lived experiences begin to interweave into the content you are unpacking. This is the step where disciplined action takes root and gives form to observable results.

Upon your subsequent reading of the script allow your mind to reveal the meaning of the carefully crafted words. Release your pride and allow your awareness to show you where you lack and show you where you excel related to each leadership insight.

Disciplined action takes root and gives form to observable results.

Third...
On Friday, write down what you have learned about the week's insight script. Capture how you have come to understand this law of leadership. Address how you will incorporate this insight into the remainder of your tenure as a leader. Reflective leaders are effective leaders.

Reflective leaders are effective leaders.

Fourth...
Repeat steps one through three for each script in your possession. Address only one script per week.

May your leadership-changing journey begin, now.

2
ATTITUDE

Attitude is the lever by which leaders impact their employees and organization, and the lens through which a leader views their circumstances and environment.

A leader must recognize that attitude profoundly shapes a leader's impact. Attitudes are powerful as they influence a leaders' beliefs, feelings, actions, and responses. Attitude influences how you view your team members, execute policies, approach challenges, cast vision, build relationships, and foster collaboration.

The attitude lens of a leader is not about constant positivity. The attitude lens of a leader is about consciously choosing how to view and respond to circumstances. No matter what is happening around you, your attitude remains within your control. Conscious awareness of, and conscious cultivation of, your attitude is essential for effective leadership.

Four practical ways to consciously cultivate your attitude are:
1. ***Gratitude***: Take time each day to reflect on what you're grateful for. Acknowledge small victories, appreciate the present moment, and focus on the positives.

2. ***Inner Dialogue***: Be aware of your inner dialogue. Inner dialogue is the ongoing stream of thoughts and conversations that occur within your own mind. This internal monologue can encompass a wide range of reflections, from analyzing situations and making decisions to rehearsing conversations and processing emotions. Replace all negative inner dialogue. Inner dialogue can instantly alter attitude.

3. ***Associations***: Surround yourself with positive associations. Attitude is contagious, so take caution with whom you let into your circle of influence.

4. ***Reframe***: Challenges and setbacks are inevitable.

> Reframe challenges and setbacks as opportunities for growth. Opportunities for a shift in direction or approach. Opportunities for inspired change.

Remember, attitude impacts all aspects of your life and influences how you show up as a leader. Attitude is malleable – attitude is controllable - it is based on choice and decision not circumstance and environment.

Attitude profoundly shapes your leadership impact.

Leader Insights: Leadership Essentials to Inspire and Guide

Reading Tracker

☐ Monday ☐ Tuesday ☐ Wednesday ☐ Thursday ☐ Friday

Leader Reflection

Reflecting on what you've read is a great way to deepen your understanding and apply new insights.

1) **How can I integrate this leadership principle into my current leadership approach?** Think about specific strategies or behaviors mentioned and how you can adapt them to your own style.

_____
_____
_____

2) **What are the key challenges I face as a leader, and how can this concept help me address them?** Identify any recurring obstacles in your leadership role and consider how the new knowledge can provide solutions or improvements.

_____
_____
_____

3) **How do my leadership strengths and weaknesses align with this leadership concept?** Assess your own skills and areas for growth in relation to the content, and plan actionable steps to enhance your leadership effectiveness.

_____
_____
_____
_____

Leader Insights: Leadership Essentials to Inspire and Guide

3
MOTIVATION

As a leader, your ability to motivate your team directly impacts their performance, their engagement, their job satisfaction, and their overall success.

Motivation of others – the degree to which they are motivated – determines what they are willing to do, what actions they will do, and how long they will persevere in the face of difficulty.

Defined, motivation is anything which instigates one to engage in a particular behavior to satisfy a specific internal state.

Instigating, or unlocking, motivation in others is paramount for a leader.

Here are three key principles to keep in mind:

1) **D.N.A**: Recognize that motivation varies from person to person. Some employees thrive on external recognition and rewards (extrinsic motivation), such as bonuses or promotions, while others find fulfillment in the work itself (intrinsic motivation). Take the time to understand what drives each team member. Think of it as finding out their unique D.N.A – Desires, Needs, and Aims. When you can come to understand each employees' desires, needs, and aims – you will understand what motivates them.

2) *Motivating Climate*: Foster a workplace climate where motivation has the opportunity to flourish. A workplace environment where employees feel valued, respected, connected, and increasingly realizing their potential. Often, the greatest thing you can do as a leader is create the environment in which motivation can take place.

3) *Clear Goals and Expectations*: Ambiguity of goals and expectations can lead to intermittent motivation, and lack of clear vision can lead to demotivation. Clearly define expectations and articulate clear and

achievable goals. When employees understand their role, have a clear path forward, and see how they impact overall success, they are more likely to stay motivated.

Effective leaders put in the effort to understand individual motivations, create a motivating environment, and set clear goals and expectations with others. By doing so, you'll inspire your team to perform at their best and continue to contribute to organizational success.

Motivation determines willingness, actions, and perseverance.

Leader Insights: Leadership Essentials to Inspire and Guide

Reading Tracker

☐ Monday ☐ Tuesday ☐ Wednesday ☐ Thursday ☐ Friday

Leader Reflection

Reflecting on what you've read is a great way to deepen your understanding and apply new insights.

1) **How can I integrate this leadership principle into my current leadership approach?** Think about specific strategies or behaviors mentioned and how you can adapt them to your own style.

   _____
   _____
   _____
   _____

2) **What are the key challenges I face as a leader, and how can this concept help me address them?** Identify any recurring obstacles in your leadership role and consider how the new knowledge can provide solutions or improvements.

   _____
   _____
   _____
   _____

3) **How do my leadership strengths and weaknesses align with this leadership concept?** Assess your own skills and areas for growth in relation to the content, and plan actionable steps to enhance your leadership effectiveness.

   _____
   _____
   _____
   _____

Leader Insights: Leadership Essentials to Inspire and Guide

4
ACCOUNTABILITY

Leaders understand that holding themselves accountable for decisions and actions establishes a foundation of trust and credibility within the organization and their team members. When leaders model accountability, they inspire their teams to do the same, fostering a culture of ownership and dependability.

Accountability (both for yourself and those you lead) is crucial for successful leadership. Accountability manifests itself as ownership of the outcome, regardless of the circumstances. Effective accountability fosters trust, collaboration, and a results-driven culture.

Here are some practical strategies for creating an environment of accountability:

- ***Clear Expectations***: Set, and clearly communicate, expectations and standards. Ensure team members understand their roles, responsibilities, desired outcomes, and how performance and success will be measured. You cannot hold others accountable to something of which they were not aware.

- ***Regular Check-Ins***: Schedule regular one-on-one meetings to discuss progress, address challenges, and provide feedback to each team member. Check-ins demonstrate commitment to accountability and create a mechanism for the "system" to keep accountability front and center.

- ***Consequences and Rewards***: Implement consequences for missed targets or poor performance. Of course, these will be unique to your organization and your team. Equally, recognize and reward achievements. Consistency of consequences and rewards is critical for long-term accountability across all team members.

- ***Constructive Feedback***: Provide specific, actionable

feedback on behaviors, actions, and outcomes. Through your feedback, encourage continuous growth and movement toward the desired outcomes.

Accountability breeds trust by emphasizing responsibility, commitment, and ownership. Demonstrating accountability in your own actions - model responsibility and ownership - sets the tone for the entire team.

Accountability manifests itself as ownership of the outcome, regardless of the circumstances.

Reading Tracker

☐ Monday ☐ Tuesday ☐ Wednesday ☐ Thursday ☐ Friday

Leader Reflection

Reflecting on what you've read is a great way to deepen your understanding and apply new insights.

1) **How can I integrate this leadership principle into my current leadership approach?** Think about specific strategies or behaviors mentioned and how you can adapt them to your own style.

   _____
   _____
   _____
   _____

2) **What are the key challenges I face as a leader, and how can this concept help me address them?** Identify any recurring obstacles in your leadership role and consider how the new knowledge can provide solutions or improvements.

   _____
   _____
   _____
   _____

3) **How do my leadership strengths and weaknesses align with this leadership concept?** Assess your own skills and areas for growth in relation to the content, and plan actionable steps to enhance your leadership effectiveness.

   _____
   _____
   _____
   _____

5
COACHING THROUGH LISTENING

A critical component of coaching employees for improved performance is active listening.

Active listening is the key to unlocking employee potential. As a leader, your ability to actively listen is a decisive asset. One that many leaders do not utilize regularly. The true power of active listening is found in putting it into practice.

Active listening is not just about hearing; it's about focusing, connecting, and responding to ensure mutual understanding. Employing active listening actually empowers employees to reach their full potential.

Here are four practical strategies for active listening:

1) ***Understanding Perspectives***: Active listening involves not only hearing what employees say but also understanding their perspectives and emotions. By truly grasping their viewpoints, you build trust and rapport, creating an environment conducive to safety and growth. Through true listening, seek understanding of other's perspectives.

2) ***Engage All The Senses***: Active listening – when used correctly – is an act of authenticity. Engaging all your senses while interacting with team members deepens the connection. Listen not only to their words but also tune into their emotions, body language, and unspoken cues. Assimilate each element and savor how they blend to create a full sense of perspective of the other person. Listen with all senses engaged.

3) ***Practice Curiosity***: Curiosity is the fuel for active listening. When you are genuinely curious, listening becomes the dominant skill, and employees feel valued and understood. Curiosity manifests as exploration of the other person's perspectives, feelings, and ideas – which results in deep understanding. Practice curiosity.

4) ***Listen Strategically:*** Listen for themes, patterns, and deeper meanings. Develop the ability to discern desires, biases, and concerns—the unspoken layers beneath their words. What is expressed with mere words is only one avenue of exploration. What is expressed with emotions, body, tone, rate, pitch, pauses is another avenue. What is unsaid is yet another avenue of exploration. Listen strategically to all avenues of meaning.

Active listening is a skill that must be honed through use, and use alone. Don't let your familiarity with the term 'active listening' fool you into thinking you are an active listener. Active listening is a tool in which the use will yield understanding, empathy, perspective, and skillful guidance.

Active listening is an authentic act which yields true understanding.

Leader Insights: Leadership Essentials to Inspire and Guide

Reading Tracker

☐ Monday ☐ Tuesday ☐ Wednesday ☐ Thursday ☐ Friday

Leader Reflection

Reflecting on what you've read is a great way to deepen your understanding and apply new insights.

1) **How can I integrate this leadership principle into my current leadership approach?** Think about specific strategies or behaviors mentioned and how you can adapt them to your own style.

___

___

___

2) **What are the key challenges I face as a leader, and how can this concept help me address them?** Identify any recurring obstacles in your leadership role and consider how the new knowledge can provide solutions or improvements.

___

___

___

3) **How do my leadership strengths and weaknesses align with this leadership concept?** Assess your own skills and areas for growth in relation to the content, and plan actionable steps to enhance your leadership effectiveness.

___

___

___

___

6
FEEDBACK

Providing effective feedback is a crucial responsibility for any leader.

Feedback serves as a catalyst for growth. When leaders provide impactful feedback, team members gain insights into their capabilities and level of competence in a given task. Regular feedback helps individuals continuously refine their skills, adapt to changing circumstances, and enhance their overall performance.

A person does not fully understand their level of competence until he or she begins to perform and receives the first glimpse of feedback. It is at this point that people report the psychological experience of understanding their true level of competence for a given task. That's the power of feedback.

Impactful feedback is specific, actionable, and timely. When feedback is too vague and not actionable then no behavior change will result. And, waiting too long can diminish its impact. Whether it's praise or corrective feedback, deliver it as close to the observed behavior as possible. This ensures that team members can connect the feedback to their specific actions and behaviors.

Many leaders overlook the fact that feedback comes from multiple sources, not just from evaluation from the leader to the team member. Additional sources of feedback which an effective leader will exploit are:
1) Feedback from the task itself. This one is often overlooked in a feedback session – what is the task itself telling you about your capabilities and your level of competence.
2) Comparison of one's current performance with one's past performance.
3) Comparison of one's current performance with the performance of others.

Leaders who tap into all sources of feedback and prioritize

feedback create a culture of continuous learning, boost morale, and drive team success. Remember to be specific, action-oriented, and timely in your feedback approach.

Feedback, which is specific, actionable, and timely is a catalyst for individual growth.

Reading Tracker

☐ Monday ☐ Tuesday ☐ Wednesday ☐ Thursday ☐ Friday

Leader Reflection

Reflecting on what you've read is a great way to deepen your understanding and apply new insights.

1) **How can I integrate this leadership principle into my current leadership approach?** Think about specific strategies or behaviors mentioned and how you can adapt them to your own style.

   _____
   _____
   _____
   _____

2) **What are the key challenges I face as a leader, and how can this concept help me address them?** Identify any recurring obstacles in your leadership role and consider how the new knowledge can provide solutions or improvements.

   _____
   _____
   _____
   _____

3) **How do my leadership strengths and weaknesses align with this leadership concept?** Assess your own skills and areas for growth in relation to the content, and plan actionable steps to enhance your leadership effectiveness.

   _____
   _____
   _____
   _____

7
COLLABORATION

Your actions as a leader set the tone for collaboration for the entire team. By nurturing collaboration, you will create a more productive and harmonious work environment.

The essence of collaboration is people working together to achieve common goals. It involves sharing knowledge, skills, and ideas to enhance productivity and innovation.

When you create an environment where collaboration is encouraged you will realize:

- ***Better Problem-Solving***: A leader who influences a collaborative environment allows team members to generate more solutions to a given problem, refine solutions, and find creative approaches to challenges.

- ***Individual Development***: When people collaborate, they learn from one another, expand their skill sets, and grow both personally and professionally.

- ***Sense of Belonging***: A leader who influences a collaborative environment fosters a positive work environment where team members feel connected, valued, and part of a cohesive unit. This sense of belonging extends into a sense of safety, which in turn leads to more freedom to be creative and innovative.

- ***Strengths-based Task Division***: By creating a collaborative environment, teams can safely divide tasks based on individual strengths, leading to more efficient execution and successful outcomes.

But, not all leaders know the keys to creating a collaborative environment. Read each key and consider how you can include them in your leadership approach.

- ***Key #1. Establish Clear Objectives***: Begin by defining the purpose and desired outcomes for your team. When everyone aligns around a common objective, collaboration becomes more effective. Think of it as charting a course—the clearer the destination, the smoother the journey.

- ***Key #2. Encourage Open Communication:*** Imagine your team as a symphony orchestra. Each instrument plays a unique part, but they harmonize to create beautiful music. Similarly, create an environment where team members feel safe and comfortable sharing their ideas, concerns, and feedback.

- ***Key #3. Promote Trust and Psychological Safety:*** Trust is the bedrock of collaboration. Like a bridge connecting two shores, trust allows people to cross safely. As a leader, foster an atmosphere where team members feel safe to take risks, express themselves, and learn from their mistakes. When trust exists, collaboration flows naturally.

You, as the leader, can create an environment where collaboration is present. Don't undermine your influence on this important element of your team.

When leaders establish clear objectives, encourage open communication, and promote trust and psychological safety, the result is a collaborative team.

Reading Tracker
☐ Monday ☐ Tuesday ☐ Wednesday ☐ Thursday ☐ Friday

Leader Reflection

Reflecting on what you've read is a great way to deepen your understanding and apply new insights.

1) **How can I integrate this leadership principle into my current leadership approach?** Think about specific strategies or behaviors mentioned and how you can adapt them to your own style.

_____
_____
_____

2) **What are the key challenges I face as a leader, and how can this concept help me address them?** Identify any recurring obstacles in your leadership role and consider how the new knowledge can provide solutions or improvements.

_____
_____
_____

3) **How do my leadership strengths and weaknesses align with this leadership concept?** Assess your own skills and areas for growth in relation to the content, and plan actionable steps to enhance your leadership effectiveness.

_____
_____
_____
_____

8
TRUST

Trust is the bedrock upon which successful leadership stands. As a leader, your actions will either cultivate trust or erode trust. It truly is an "either / or" phenomena. Trust is a silent architect that is responsible for designing and building successful leaders. Silent, in that, so few leaders understand its impact and power.

Think of trust as the currency of modern-day leadership. Trust is deposited and withdrawn from the social and emotional account of each employe on your team, with each and every interaction you have.

Here are practical ways that leaders can foster trust:

- ***Be Trusting***: Be the first to trust others. The act of trusting, it seems, increases trust in all parties. Levels of trust increase in people who act in a trusting manner and in people who are trusted. Be the first to trust.

- ***Be Transparent***: Share information openly and candidly. Keep your team updated on company matters and decisions made.

- ***Demonstrate Expertise***: Show competence and good judgment. When your team sees that you know what you are doing, they will be more likely to trust your decisions.

- ***Listen and Respond with Empathy***: Actively listen to your team members. Understand their concerns and respond with empathy. This builds a sense of connection which influences trust.

- ***Acknowledge Your Own Failures***: Although you are to demonstrate expertise and show your competence, you must also be genuine about your own mistakes as a leader. When leaders admit their errors, it humanizes you and fosters trust.

- ***Demonstrate Integrity and Fairness***: Uphold ethical standards. Treat everyone fairly and transparently. Trust flourishes when leaders act with integrity.

Trust is the foundation of strong leadership, and these practices contribute to a positive and productive work culture.

If a leader is not consciously considering *how* they are cultivating trust, and are not intentional *about* cultivating trust, it will be evident to all observers within the team and organization.

Trust, the silent architect of leadership, it shapes success. Cultivate it wisely.

Reading Tracker

☐ Monday ☐ Tuesday ☐ Wednesday ☐ Thursday ☐ Friday

Leader Reflection

Reflecting on what you've read is a great way to deepen your understanding and apply new insights.

1) **How can I integrate this leadership principle into my current leadership approach?** Think about specific strategies or behaviors mentioned and how you can adapt them to your own style.

   _____
   _____
   _____
   _____

2) **What are the key challenges I face as a leader, and how can this concept help me address them?** Identify any recurring obstacles in your leadership role and consider how the new knowledge can provide solutions or improvements.

   _____
   _____
   _____
   _____

3) **How do my leadership strengths and weaknesses align with this leadership concept?** Assess your own skills and areas for growth in relation to the content, and plan actionable steps to enhance your leadership effectiveness.

   _____
   _____
   _____
   _____

9
SUPPORT SELF-EFFICACY

Leadership is about empowering the performance of others to use their skills, abilities, and capabilities, to successfully achieve a common vision.

Leaders know that one critical element can make or break the achievement of the vision – an employee's belief in their ability to achieve. In other words, the employee's self-efficacy.

Self-efficacy refers to an individual's belief in their ability to accomplish specific tasks or goals. It's the confidence they have in their own competence and capacity to succeed. In short, it is the answer to the question that all employees ask of themselves, "can I do this?"

Four reasons why Self-Efficacy is critical for employee success:

1) ***Performance and Persistence***: Employees with high self-efficacy are more likely to take on challenging tasks and persist in their efforts. They believe they can overcome obstacles, leading to improved performance.

2) ***Motivation and Effort***: When employees feel confident in their abilities, they invest more effort. Self-efficacy acts as a motivational force, driving them to achieve their best.

3) ***Task Selection and Goal Setting***: Self-efficacy influences the tasks employees choose to learn and the goals they set for themselves. It guides their focus and direction.

4) ***Coping with Challenges***: In the face of challenges, those with a high self-efficacy are more willing to put in the extra effort needed to cope effectively. It's like having an in-built reservoir of resilience and problem-solving skills.

What can you do as a leader to support Self-Efficacy? Here are two sources of self-efficacy influence to use with your employees:

1) ***Mastery Experience***: This is, perhaps, the most influential source of self-efficacy. Simply, it is gaining confidence in one's abilities by successfully completing tasks and achieving goals. So, a) create opportunities for success that ladder into additional successes for your employees; and b) support your employees when placing them in situations where they are likely to fail at first.

2) ***Vicarious Learning***: Observing others, who are similar to oneself, succeed in performing a given task can increase self-efficacy. This observation can bolster one's belief in their won capability to perform the same task. So, a) provide examples of what success looks like, and b) guide employees to collaborate with more capable peers in order to witness the successful behavior in action.

Leaders, nurture self-efficacy in your team. When employees believe in their ability to succeed at the given task or goal, they soar to new heights in performance, overcome hurdles, and contribute significantly to organizational outcomes.

The greatest influence factor on the performance of your team members is how they individually answer the question, "can I do this?"

Reading Tracker

☐ Monday ☐ Tuesday ☐ Wednesday ☐ Thursday ☐ Friday

Leader Reflection

Reflecting on what you've read is a great way to deepen your understanding and apply new insights.

1) **How can I integrate this leadership principle into my current leadership approach?** Think about specific strategies or behaviors mentioned and how you can adapt them to your own style.

   _____
   _____
   _____
   _____

2) **What are the key challenges I face as a leader, and how can this concept help me address them?** Identify any recurring obstacles in your leadership role and consider how the new knowledge can provide solutions or improvements.

   _____
   _____
   _____
   _____

3) **How do my leadership strengths and weaknesses align with this leadership concept?** Assess your own skills and areas for growth in relation to the content, and plan actionable steps to enhance your leadership effectiveness.

   _____
   _____
   _____
   _____

10
CHANGE

Change is inevitable in today's dynamic business landscape. Simply put, change is a movement out of a current state (how things are today), through a transition state, into a future state (how things will be).

As much as organizations need to commit to constant change to keep up with the dynamic business landscape, they need employees who are committed to being flexible, adaptable, and embracing change.

Your role as a leader extends beyond merely implementing change; it involves reducing the resistance to change and guiding your team through the transition state, into the future state. Resistance is a normal human response to change and requires an effective leader to guide the organization and their teams through the change process. Teams who navigate change successfully have leaders who anticipate change, prepare for change, and fully commit to change.

Here are three key principles to keep in mind:

1) ***Embrace and Demonstrate a Growth Attitude***: Since your team will be looking at how you embrace or resist change, demonstrate that you understand how change is essential for organizational growth. Rather than resisting change, model how you have cultivated a positive attitude toward change. In turn, your team will follow your lead.

2) ***Continuously Communicate the Change***: Know there is fear and uncertainty in the change journey for your team members. This is a normal human response with any change. True leaders communicate through those fears and uncertainties. Successful change leaders work through the resistance by communicating answers to the questions that are swirling around the heads of their employees. Answering questions like: What is changing? What's not changing? Why is it changing? Why is it changing now? What happens if we don't change?

3) ***Focus on People and Process***: Effective change leadership requires a balance between process and people. That balance expresses itself through: a) communicating purposefully, b) connecting the change to organizational values AND the individuals' values, c) involving team members in the change, d) breaking down complex changes into smaller, manageable pieces, and e) celebrating successes along the way.

Purposeful change-leadership, by fostering a growth attitude and focusing on both people and processes related to change, will reduce resistance to change and will bolster acceptance of the change.

Teams who navigate change successfully have leaders who anticipate change, prepare for change, and fully commit to change.

Reading Tracker

☐ Monday ☐ Tuesday ☐ Wednesday ☐ Thursday ☐ Friday

Leader Reflection

Reflecting on what you've read is a great way to deepen your understanding and apply new insights.

1) **How can I integrate this leadership principle into my current leadership approach?** Think about specific strategies or behaviors mentioned and how you can adapt them to your own style.

_____
_____
_____
_____

2) **What are the key challenges I face as a leader, and how can this concept help me address them?** Identify any recurring obstacles in your leadership role and consider how the new knowledge can provide solutions or improvements.

_____
_____
_____
_____

3) **How do my leadership strengths and weaknesses align with this leadership concept?** Assess your own skills and areas for growth in relation to the content, and plan actionable steps to enhance your leadership effectiveness.

_____
_____
_____
_____

11
INFLUENCE

Influence is a critical factor in effective leadership. As a leader, your ability to influence others enables you to inspire, motivate, and guide your team toward success. It also plays a pivotal role in creating a positive organizational culture that promotes teamwork, innovation, and growth.

There are a few secret sources of influence a leader must discover and utilize in order to effectively influence action and movement of others:

1. ***Personal Motivation and Personal Ability***: help team members connect their individual actions to their core values and aspirations. This leads to more consistent motivation. Additionally, assesses whether an individual has the capability to perform the desired behavior. When the answer is "yes" they are more likely to move in the direction of your influence.

2. ***Social Motivation and Social Ability***: harness peer support and create an environment where others encourage the right behaviors. Ethical social influence is a powerful tool within the hands of a leader. Additionally, foster a supportive community where team members provide help, share information, and offer resources to ensure collective efforts amplify individual abilities.

Influence isn't about control; it's about ethically inspiring positive change, impacting performance, and empowering those around you by understanding motivation and ability in the personal and social realms.

Influence is crucial for effective leadership; it empowers leaders to inspire, guide, and create positive change within their teams and their organizations.

Influence taps into personal and social motivation and ability in order to inspire guided action.

Reading Tracker

☐ Monday ☐ Tuesday ☐ Wednesday ☐ Thursday ☐ Friday

Leader Reflection

Reflecting on what you've read is a great way to deepen your understanding and apply new insights.

1) **How can I integrate this leadership principle into my current leadership approach?** Think about specific strategies or behaviors mentioned and how you can adapt them to your own style.

   _____
   _____
   _____
   _____

2) **What are the key challenges I face as a leader, and how can this concept help me address them?** Identify any recurring obstacles in your leadership role and consider how the new knowledge can provide solutions or improvements.

   _____
   _____
   _____
   _____

3) **How do my leadership strengths and weaknesses align with this leadership concept?** Assess your own skills and areas for growth in relation to the content, and plan actionable steps to enhance your leadership effectiveness.

   _____
   _____
   _____
   _____

Leader Insights: Leadership Essentials to Inspire and Guide

12
RADICAL IMPROVEMENT

Leaders know the power of continuous improvement. But, only a few leaders explore the power of radical improvements.

Radical improvements make a quantum leap between current state and future state. Radical improvements set the aim a few clicks higher than what is comfortable. Radical improvements expedite performance and goal achievement.

Here are four elements for accelerating performance and creating radical improvements:

1. ***Ambitious Aim***: Radical improvement sets a new aiming point—a higher plane than what currently exists. You must define ambitious goals that stretch your team's capabilities and push them beyond the familiar horizon.

2. ***Relentless Pursuit***: Radical improvements demand persistent commitment from the team. It demands the pursuit of goals with intensity. The pursuit will be uncomfortable, but one must keep pushing forward and embrace discomfort. Discomfort is a sign you are on the right track, a sign you are making progress toward something new, something radical.

3. ***Sweeping Shift***: Radical improvement starts with a sweeping shift of your mind and attitude toward what is possible. One must come to understand that one's mindset shapes one's reality. Radical improvement requires one to cultivate mental agility; to replace self-limiting beliefs with empowering beliefs, growth-oriented beliefs; and to vividly visualize success on this new plane. A sweeping shift of your mind fuels radical improvement.

4. ***Meticulous Monitoring***: Radical improvements requires regular assessment of progress. Regular assessment requires meticulous monitoring of

progress. Defined and articulated metrics and milestones will allow data-driven insights to track how close you are to the radical improvement.

As a leader, you must tap into the power of radical improvements and inspire your team to embrace these principles and achieve exponential gains. Inspire your team with radical improvements and watch performance soar!

Radical improvements push your team past the familiar horizon onto a new plane of success.

Reading Tracker

☐ Monday ☐ Tuesday ☐ Wednesday ☐ Thursday ☐ Friday

Leader Reflection

Reflecting on what you've read is a great way to deepen your understanding and apply new insights.

1) **How can I integrate this leadership principle into my current leadership approach?** Think about specific strategies or behaviors mentioned and how you can adapt them to your own style.

   _____
   _____
   _____
   _____

2) **What are the key challenges I face as a leader, and how can this concept help me address them?** Identify any recurring obstacles in your leadership role and consider how the new knowledge can provide solutions or improvements.

   _____
   _____
   _____
   _____

3) **How do my leadership strengths and weaknesses align with this leadership concept?** Assess your own skills and areas for growth in relation to the content, and plan actionable steps to enhance your leadership effectiveness.

   _____
   _____
   _____
   _____

13
MODEL THE WAY

As a leader, you must embody the behaviors, values, and actions you expect from your employees. Human nature is such that in the absence of clearly defined expectations, employees create their own expectations. A leader not only verbalizes the way (the expectations), but also models the way (the expected behaviors, attitudes, and norms).

When you model the way for your team you are demonstrating authenticity and integrity. Your actions as a leader truly speak louder than your words. Whether it is adhering to ethical standards, showing resilience, or embracing change, your actions and behaviors set the standard for everyone else.

When you model the way for your team you are demonstrating what you value. Your core values are the guiding principles that drive your decisions and actions. Modeling the way makes your core values evident to all, as your behaviors will always follow your values. Whether you are intentional about modeling the way or not intentional, your actions and behaviors WILL be the model to which your team members measure what is expected and what is permissible.

When you model the way for your team you are demonstrating what "right" looks like. You are the role model your team needs. When you exemplify commitment, dedication, work ethic, balance, attitude, and the like, your team members will follow.

True leaders understand that, for good or for bad, they are the models for their employees and their organization. What you do, as a leader, becomes the way for your team.

Regardless of your intention, your actions and behaviors WILL be the model to which your team members measure what is expected and what is permissible.

Reading Tracker

☐ Monday ☐ Tuesday ☐ Wednesday ☐ Thursday ☐ Friday

Leader Reflection

Reflecting on what you've read is a great way to deepen your understanding and apply new insights.

1) **How can I integrate this leadership principle into my current leadership approach?** Think about specific strategies or behaviors mentioned and how you can adapt them to your own style.

___
___
___

2) **What are the key challenges I face as a leader, and how can this concept help me address them?** Identify any recurring obstacles in your leadership role and consider how the new knowledge can provide solutions or improvements.

___
___
___

3) **How do my leadership strengths and weaknesses align with this leadership concept?** Assess your own skills and areas for growth in relation to the content, and plan actionable steps to enhance your leadership effectiveness.

___
___
___
___

Leader Insights: Leadership Essentials to Inspire and Guide

14
CAST VISION

Vision casting is the strategic process whereby leaders communicate an inspiring, vivid, and clear picture of what the future could look like for the team and the organization. Said another way, vision casting is the art of conveying a detailed, captivating, and motivating picture of what future success looks like and feels like when achieved.

Effective vision casting involves three essential components:

- ***The Picture***: You must paint a vivid, captivating, compelling, and inspiring picture which engages both logic and emotion. You must craft a compelling narrative around your vision through the use of storytelling to engage emotions and create a sense of urgency. Your picture will be the influence for inspiring employees and stakeholders to join in the pursuit of the vision.

- ***The Purpose***: The vision must encapsulate the fundamental principles that guide the future decision making to align with the vision, and the team's reason for continuous persistence toward the vision (beyond making profit). The purpose is the "compass" that directs the vision and points to the true north in face of obstacles.

- ***The Performance***: The vision must articulate what behaviors and performance expectations are necessary to reach the inspiring target. In many cases these behavior and performance expectations will be considered stretch capabilities, so ensure the necessary support mechanisms (training programs, technology, processes, and manager capabilities) are in place to support the required behaviors and performance.

Vision casting isn't a one-time event—it's an ongoing process. As a leader, revisit and refine your vision regularly, ensuring it remains relevant, inspiring, and top of mind. Vision casting is an essential tool for leaders to map out the future of their organization. Picture, purpose, and performance are the foundational elements to create a solid base for the vision. By mastering vision casting, leaders can inspire their teams toward a common goal and propel the organization into the future.

Vision casting is the art of conveying the picture, the purpose, and the performance in a captivating and motivating manner.

Leader Insights: Leadership Essentials to Inspire and Guide

Reading Tracker

☐ Monday ☐ Tuesday ☐ Wednesday ☐ Thursday ☐ Friday

Leader Reflection

Reflecting on what you've read is a great way to deepen your understanding and apply new insights.

1) **How can I integrate this leadership principle into my current leadership approach?** Think about specific strategies or behaviors mentioned and how you can adapt them to your own style.

   _____
   _____
   _____

2) **What are the key challenges I face as a leader, and how can this concept help me address them?** Identify any recurring obstacles in your leadership role and consider how the new knowledge can provide solutions or improvements.

   _____
   _____
   _____

3) **How do my leadership strengths and weaknesses align with this leadership concept?** Assess your own skills and areas for growth in relation to the content, and plan actionable steps to enhance your leadership effectiveness.

   _____
   _____
   _____
   _____

When you exhaust the scripts...
As you execute the steps described in this pamphlet, you will eventually exhaust all the insight scripts. This means, dear Leader, that you have journeyed to a place in your leadership growth which few have dared to go. This means you have pushed past a cursory knowledge of humans and leadership and motivation and awareness into a realm of true understanding. And, it is in that understanding that your actions manifest and bring life to the laws that govern effective leadership.

NOTES:

NOTES:

NOTES:

NOTES:

NOTES:

NOTES:

NOTES:

NOTES:

ABOUT THE AUTHOR

Dr. Corey Pruitt

Speaker. Author. Human Performance Strategist. Learning Experience Architect.

Dr. Pruitt is a thought leader in the areas of leadership, learning, and human performance. His unique blend of experiences in psychology, business leadership, and higher education leadership have set the foundation for his ability to motivate and transform individuals and organizations toward growth and lasting performance improvement. With nearly 20 years of experience in leadership roles, Corey has a proven track record across multiple industries such as higher education, technology, fin/tech, and health & wellness.

Dr. Pruitt's personal philosophy is grounded in the belief that human potential is a remarkable force. He emphasizes that a true leader is dedicated to continually exploring and expanding the potential within each of their employees. This belief fuels his commitment to developing transformative leadership practices that empower individuals and organizations alike.

Corey has obtained an undergraduate degree in Human Communication, a Master's degree in Psychology, and a Doctorate in Leadership.

Additional Publications by Dr. Pruitt:

- Spark*: Provoking Radical People-Centered Innovation*
- Action From Interaction*: The Art and Science of Managing Performance Outcomes Through Communication*

Available at: www.ChangeSparx.com or Amazon.com

www.ingramcontent.com/pod-product-compliance
Lightning Source LLC
Chambersburg PA
CBHW050324230526
45471CB00005B/2338